FUTURE
SURVIVAL

FUT
SURV

The Word For Today
Costa Mesa, California

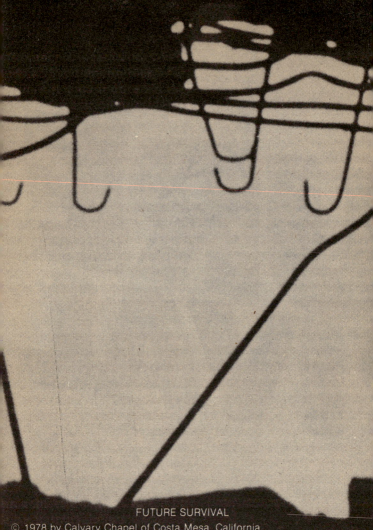

FUTURE SURVIVAL

Printed in U.S.A.   ISBN 0-936728-02-7

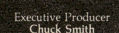

Executive Producer
Chuck Smith

Produced and Directed by
Bob Cording and Jerry Humphries

Post Production
**Brian Barkley, Magic Film Works, Anthony Bozanich
Roger Boller, David Oren**

Sound
**Maranatha Music, Michael Strong, Lester Kisling
Pelifilm Productions**

Stock Footage
Israel Film Service, Grinberg Film Library, NASA

Contents

1980's Update

As we look at the world today, we see that the stage is almost totally set for the return of Jesus Christ.

Israel Reborn

Bible prophecies clearly indicate that one of the major prerequisites and vital signs of the return of the Lord would be the reestablishment of the nation of Israel. This event has taken place within our lifetime. 1948 saw the rebirth of the nation Israel.

European Community

In addition to Israel's statehood, the Bible predicts the existence of a confederacy of European nations before the return of Christ. This confederacy would ultimately involve ten nations and become a world power.

This prediction is found in the Book of Daniel. King Nebuchadnezzar, the ruler of Babylon, had a dream about a huge image. It had a head of gold, shoulders of silver, stomach of brass, legs of iron, feet of iron and clay with ten toes.

In the interpretation of Nebuchadnezzar's dream Daniel said, "God has shown you the kingdoms of

1

the world. Before you went to sleep you were wondering what would be the end of the world and what would happen to your kingdom.

"In your dream you saw a great image of gold, silver, brass, iron, and feet of iron and clay. You, Nebuchadnezzar, are the head of gold, but your Babylonian kingdom will be replaced by the Medo-Persian empire, the shoulders of silver. That will be replaced by the Grecian empire, the stomach of brass, which will fall to the Roman empire, the legs of iron.

"The final world-governing empire will be a federation of ten nations, as represented in the mixture of iron and clay of the ten toes."

The mixture of iron and clay signifies a democracy that's related to the Roman empire. This revival of the Roman empire will rule not as one nation but as a federation of ten nations. Bible students have been looking for this, a United States of Europe, as a sign of the Second Coming for a long time.

As Nebuchadnezzar was watching this image, a rock not cut with hands came out of the mountains. The rock hit the huge image in its feet, the whole image crumbled, and the rock grew into a mountain that covered the earth. Daniel said that the rock is actually the coming of the Messiah.

When the Messiah comes He'll bring an end to men's endeavors to govern themselves. The Messiah will establish a Kingdom that will cover the whole earth and will never fall.

A world-governing empire hasn't existed since the days of the Roman empire. The British empire came close, and Hitler dreamed of world dominion.

But now nine European nations have federated as the European Community (EC). On January 1, 1981, Greece will become the tenth member nation of this federation. The new 10-nation European Community is related to the old Roman empire, has a European Parliament, a Council of Ministers, and a European president. The EC is forming the European monetary unit and plans to make it the new international medium of exchange replacing the U.S. dollar.

The stage is being set for man's final world-governing empire. You can read about the European Community in your news magazines and newspapers. God has put another part of the puzzle into place, and we see things coming together.

New Economy

The message of Nebuchadnezzar's dream was repeated to Daniel in a vision. However, Daniel didn't see the future as a great image, but as various beasts. A lion, the Babylonian kingdom, was destroyed by the bear, the Medo-Persian empire. This was destroyed by the leopard, the Grecian empire, which was destroyed by an indescribable beast, the Roman empire. From this last beast came ten horns; out of the ten horns three more horns sprung out, and out of the three horns one arose and conquered the three. The one horn spoke blasphemies. Daniel saw the same progression of world empires as Nebuchadnezzar, but he saw one man rise to absolute power over the final empire and speak against the God of heaven.

A very powerful man will rise out of the European Community. This leader will make everyone take a number upon his right hand or on his forehead (Revelation 13). No one will be able to buy or sell except he has the number on his right hand or forehead.

We're being mentally conditioned to by-pass money as a medium of exchange. Money is outdated. A few years ago an ad in the paper read, "In the beginning there was money, and it was good. But now there's a better system." We're being mentally conditioned to buy and sell with numbers. Today that number is usually represented by our credit cards. We're accustomed to the idea of using personal numbers that apply to our transactions. Soon, we'll completely forget about buying and selling with cash.

Children, the spenders of the future, are being mentally conditioned. One of the banks has been distributing a children's game with a playing board and a spinner. You move a marker according to the number the spinner points to. As you go around the board, you land on various little boxes. One box says "Help," another "Cash," another "Master Charge."

If you land on the "Cash" box, you pick a little card from the Cash Cards. One Cash Card reads, "Fly now, pay later! Pay for your airline tickets with cash? How much will you have for the rest of your trip? You better slink back three spaces." Another Cash Card says, "Tire Sale! But you're flat with no cash to spare. Drive back two spaces." Another Cash Card reads, "Where did all the money go? Darned if you know. Spent here and there without receipts. Makes it a big puzzle. Stay in place and puzzle it out." And another, "This is a stick-up! You lose all of your cash. Go back to the nearest Help."

If you land on one of the boxes marked Master Charge, then you get to pick a card from the Master Charge pile. These cards say things like, "Tire Sale! Roll down to the store and buy a set of bargain tires with your Master Charge card. Advance to the nearest Sale." Or, "This is a stick-up! Your Master Charge card is taken. Report it immediately and advance to the nearest Help. Another Master Charge card is on the way!" "Pay your monthly bills. Your Master Charge monthly bill gives you a complete record, and helps you budget better. Move ahead smartly two spaces." "A long weekend! Get in your car. With your Master Charge card the family is off to celebrate the holidays in style. Drive to the nearest Travel."

As the children play this little game, they're being mentally conditioned to think that they lose with cash and win with a credit card. They're being indoctrinated to buy with a numbered card and avoid the use of cash. This programming is taking place in *every* segment of our society. We're being mentally prepared for the time when cash is no longer a medium of exchange. All of your banking, financing, buying, and selling will be with numbers assigned to you. All your transactions will be computerized.

Currently, Allstate Savings and Loan in California offers a special service when you open up a savings account. They give you a card with a special code and a toll-free telephone number. You can call up and then punch a number for the type of bill you want to pay. You use 24 for your house bill, 22 for your water bill, etc. Then you push the buttons for the amount of your bill. If your house payment is $224.00, you punch out the 2-2-4 on your telephone. The savings and loan will automatically pay your bills for you. The charge is ten cents per bill. If you were to mail your check, you'd pay more for the stamp alone. Plus, your money draws interest until the day the amount is transferred into the account of your creditor.

The Security Bank of Seattle has offered its customers "transaction money." This goes a little further than the service from Allstate Savings and Loan. You telephone the bank, tell them the bills you want to pay, and they pay them for you automatically. You also receive a transaction card that is good in the area's department stores and supermarkets. Computer relays are set up in the stores, and you use your card just like a Master Charge — only it's an automatic check transfer card. When you use this transaction card, you never receive a bill. The bank automatically transfers the money from your account to the store's account. This new system of buying with a transaction card was tried in several smaller U.S. cities and proved successful. Seattle is the first major city to inaugurate it.

We're rapidly moving towards the cashless, checkless society. You won't have to sit down at the end of the month and write out a lot of checks and stamp a lot of envelopes anymore. You can be saved all that hassle and still get interest on your money until the time your bills are paid.

The leader who'll rise from the European Community will cause everyone small and great to take a number, and no one will be able to buy or sell except he has that number on his right hand or forehead. We already have the technology to inaugurate a cashless, checkless society. We already have the equipment, the computers, everything necessary for a new economic system already installed and operational in many of our major cities. Another piece of the puzzle is fitting in!

The time is getting very short. The Lord is coming *very* soon.

Russia, Israel, and Oil

As mentioned, one of the big pieces of the puzzle that had to be in place before the return of our Lord was the rebirth of the nation Israel. The Lord spoke through the prophet Ezekiel about the rebirth of the nation Israel. Their bones would be dry and scattered, but God would put flesh and muscle on them. God promised to bring them back into the land.

Now that the Jews are dwelling in their own land, the Lord said He'd put an evil thought into the minds of the leaders of Russia. The Soviets will join forces with Iran, Libya, Ethiopia, eastern Europe, the Balkan nations, including Turkey, and they'll invade Israel.

In January of 1980 Russia moved into Afghanistan in force. In early 1979 Iran changed from a staunch ally of Israel to an avowed enemy. By late 1979 Iranian troops were in Lebanon helping the PLO in its conflict with Israel. I received an urgent

7

message from Major Saad Haddad, the Lebanese Christian militia leader in southern Lebanon. He said, "Pray for us! Thousands of Iranians are marching towards our territory, and we must defend ourselves against them."

The world is in turmoil. Iran, a major hotbed, is extremely tense. In December of 1979 Russia began a mass movement of troops from eastern Europe towards Russia's southern border, ready to move into the Mideast. Many believe that Russia's invasion of Afghanistan is just the beginning of her offensive and is being used as a test to see whether or not the United States has the strength to stand up and resist the communists.

In Ezekiel 38 the Bible tells us that when Russia moves against Israel "the merchants of Tarshish," which would be England, and "the young lions thereof," which could conceivably include the United States, will say, "Russia, what are you doing? It isn't right for you to attack this little nation!" In 1980 the United States is threatening Russia with censure in the Security Council of the United Nations for invading Afghanistan. That's just what the U.S. will do when Russia invades Israel!

Aviation Week & Space Technology (Oct. 1, 1979) published an article entitled, "Oil Seen Spurring Soviet Mideast Move." The article reports that until 1980 Russia was an exporter of oil, but she can no longer supply her own domestic needs and will soon have to start importing. However, Russia doesn't have the U.S. dollars to buy oil on the free open market.

Studies on the world's petroleum supply by the

MAJOR HOTBED: *A mixture of Islamic devotion and political unrest draws a crowd of thousands in Tehran during 1979. (Wide World Photos)*

COMMUNIST CENTRAL: Leonid Brezhnev, Soviet communist party president since 1977, and statue of Lenin, the first USSR premier (1917-1924).

STEPPING IN: This Soviet armored personnel carrier with Russian soldier at hatch patrolled the street outside the Hotel Kabul in Kabul, Afghanistan, in early 1980. *(Wide World Photos)*

CIA, MIT, and various brain trusts anticipate Russia's oil shortages to be critical by 1982-83. This dilemma will spur Russia to move into the Middle East and take over the oil-producing nations.

According to *Aviation Week & Space Technology*, even if the OPEC nations produce as much oil as they can, they will not be able to supply the increased oil needs of the industrial nations of the world beyond 1987. Unless we drastically cut oil consumption now, there may not be enough oil produced in all the world to meet the rising needs of industrialized society by 1981-82. Major economic upheavals may take place by then, because oil won't be available at any price.

Military Gap

We know that Russia is dedicated to world conquest. As a result of her invasion of Afghanistan, President Carter said that his eyes are now open. Thank God! I pray that the president has enough sense to realize that SALT II is selling the United States down the river.

In mid-1979 the Pentagon held a special briefing session for the leaders of America's major industrial companies, and the Pentagon laid out the cold, hard facts. Russia has a decided military advantage over the United States, and as a result the U.S. is entering into a crash program to catch up.

A new radar jamming system has been developed. One plane can send out false signals that totally confuse the radars. So, a plane flying on the

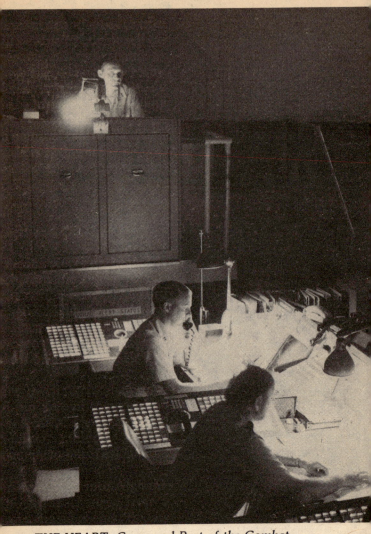

THE HEART: *Command Post of the Combat Operations Center of the North American Air Defense*

Command (NORAD) inside Cheyenne Mountain,
Colorado. (U.S. Air Force photo)

eastern side of a radar pickup tower can send signals that show up on the radar screen as a squadron of planes coming in from the west. This new technology makes radar as a detecting device practically obsolete and worthless.

The United States has developed this jamming device. We hope to have it operational by 1982. Russia already has it operational and has been jamming our radar systems in Western Europe.

We're developing multiple-particle beam weapons that have the ability to destroy electronic devices at great distances. These multiple-particle beam weapons can actually destroy satellites in orbit and shoot airplanes out of the sky. We hope to have these death-ray weapons operational by 1985. Russia already has them operational.

Russia has made tremendous advances in weaponry. The U.S. is lagging behind and cannot catch up until 1985. We hope to start closing the gap by 1983.

The Pentagon warned that 1980-82 are the most critical years for national survival in the history of the United States. Russia knows that we're entering into a crash program to regain a military balance. Therefore, Moscow is more liable to make her move into the Mideast within these two years than at any other time in history.

These are the cold, hard facts.

Wrap Up

When Jesus was talking to the disciples about His return, He said, "When you see the fig tree bud forth you know that summer is near, and you'll know that My coming is at the door. In fact," He said, "this generation will not pass until all these things be fulfilled." What generation was Jesus talking about? The generation that sees the budding of the fig tree. The budding of the fig tree represents the rebirth of the nation Israel.

In the Old Testament God often referred to Israel as His fig tree. In the New Testament Jesus came to the Mount of Olives with His disciples. He was hungry and saw a fig tree. When He went over to it, He discovered that it had no figs. He said, "Cursed be this fig tree." The next day His disciples were on the Mount of Olives again and saw that the fig tree had withered and died. They said, "Lord, that's the tree You cursed yesterday. Look how quickly it withered!"

The fig tree represents Israel. The Lord had come to the fig tree for fruit. Israel had failed to produce the fruit God was looking for. Israel had rejected the Messiah and, thus, was cursed, withered, and died. A day or so afterwards Jesus spoke on the Mount of Olives, perhaps near the same cursed fig tree. He said, "When you see the fig tree begin to bud forth, you know that summer is near, and you'll know that My coming is at the door. This generation will not pass until all these things be fulfilled."

We're the generation that saw the fig tree bud forth, as Israel became a nation again in 1948. As a rule, a generation in the Bible lasts 40 years. The children of Israel journeyed in the wilderness for 40 years until that generation died. Forty years after 1948 would bring us to 1988.

NUMBER ONE: Russia's military strength increased during the 1970s. The USSR possesses the mightiest war machine in the history of the world.

There's a 7-year prophetic period when God will again deal with the nation Israel. I cannot see the Church as being upon the earth during that period. I'm firmly convinced that the Lord will take His Church out of the world before He begins the final 7-year work with Israel. I believe that the Holy Spirit within the Church is the hindering force keeping the Antichrist from being revealed today (2 Thessalonians 2).

The moment that the Church is removed the Antichrist will rise to power, and Western Europe will then become the final world-governing empire.

This is the scenario for the last days, as I see it according to God's Word.

Western Europe, already becoming stronger every day, can never become a world empire as long as Russia remains such a powerful military force. So, as God said, "I'm going to put a hook in the jaws of the Russian bear. I'm going to bring Russia into the slaughter by bringing her into the Mideast against Israel." Russia feels that the conquest of Israel and the Mideast will be her first strategic move to world conquest.

Actually, if Russia takes the oil-producing countries of the Mideast she'll never have to fire a rocket at the United States. We can't resist or defend ourselves without the Mideast oil. We'll be so economically and industrially weakened by the loss of petroleum that we'll be at Russia's knees.

Knowing the world's dependence upon the Mideast oil, Russia feels that the wisest strategy is to move into the Middle East and take it. This way she'll avoid a nuclear holocaust and won't have to rebuild the world's industries. Russia will just take the oil and then dictate to the world. That's Russia's strategy, but that's her fatal blunder.

When Russia gets into Israel, God said that His fury will rise in His face and He'll destroy the invading Russian army. After God destroys this mighty military force Western Europe will step in as the final world-governing empire. Its leader will establish the new monetary system, and people will be buying and selling with numbers. The dominoes will begin to fall as the events move in quick progressive order during these last seven years.

From my understanding of biblical prophecies, I'm convinced that the Lord is coming for His Church before the end of 1981. I could be wrong, but it's a deep conviction in my heart, and all my plans are predicated upon that belief.

In 1986 Halley's comet is coming again. Jesus said that prior to His return in glory with His Church there'd be signs in the heavens. Halley's comet could be one of those signs in the heavens. The U.S. government has ordered a special study of the comet's orbit, because this time it will make a closer approach to the earth than at any previous time. The experts are studying the orbit to determine how close the comet will come to us. They don't expect a collision, but they fear that all this garbage in the tail of Halley's comet, which stretches out one million miles, will give the earth an incredible meteorite shower.

The possibility of debris from Halley's comet pelting the earth in 1986 is a major concern, because it could be enough to drastically affect the balance of the earth's ozone blanket. As a result, the sun's ultraviolet rays would begin to scorch people upon the earth.

The ozone blanket protects us from the sun's ultraviolet rays. Through man's use of fluorocarbon gases the ozone blanket is being depleted. The United States has outlawed the use of fluorocarbons, but the rest of the world is still using them. As the ozone blanket is being damaged, people are contracting more skin cancers from ultraviolet radiation. I received an ultraviolet radiation rash at an outdoor baptismal service in 1979. It took a few weeks for that rash to go away. Stepping out in the sunlight is becoming more dangerous every year!

The Lord said that towards the end of the Tribulation period the sun would scorch men who dwell upon the face of the earth (Rev. 16). The year 1986 would fit just about right!

We're getting *close* to the Tribulation and the return of Jesus Christ in glory!

All the pieces of the puzzle are coming together. God is warning you. Jesus rebuked the Pharisees, "You can discern the signs of the heavens, but you don't know the time of My coming. When it's evening and the sky is red you say that tomorrow will be a good day. In the morning when the sky is red you say that there'll be a storm today." Jesus said, "You blind fools! You can read the signs of the weather, but you don't the signs of My coming!"

Paul the apostle wrote to the Thessalonian Christians concerning the coming of the Lord. "You aren't children of darkness that that day should overtake you as a thief. You're the children of light." Christ's return shouldn't come as a surprise to the child of God. God has given us plenty of evidence to look for — and that evidence is here now! We can see it! And so, with Paul the apostle I say to you that all of our futures are foreshortened. We don't have time to be involved in nonessential things. The time has come to let out all the stops and go for it — because our Lord is coming very soon!

FUTURE SURVIVAL

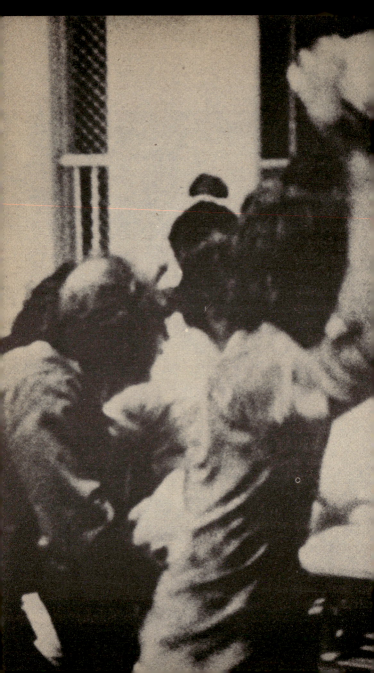

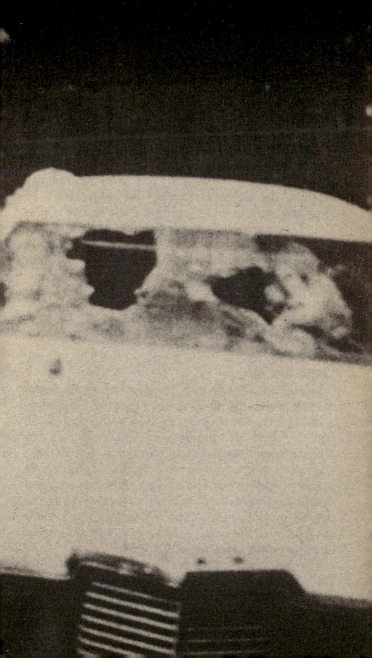

Announcer:

There are many disturbing factors in the world today that deeply concern thinking men. The population explosion, the ozone depletion, the widespread use of pesticides, pollution, the dwindling energy supplies, the threat of famine, the new staph and virus strains, the crime epidemic, the moral breakdown, plus the ever-present threat of global nuclear war. Any one of these factors pose a threat to man's survival. The question is, which one will strike first? Is there any hope for man's survival? Only a person with all the facts can be optimistic about the future.

In the next hour you will be meeting with doctors, professors, scientists, world leaders, and Chuck Smith, author and teacher, who is our special host.

Chuck Smith:

I'm Chuck Smith, and I'm also concerned about man's survival on this planet. For many years I've been studying the sociological trends, the population patterns, and the environmental conditions ... as man has been living so thoughtlessly, as though there were no tomorrow. It is rather frightening to realize that he might awake one of these mornings and find there is no tomorrow. We have carelessly wasted the natural resources that God has given unto us. We have sown to the wind—and now the time has come when we must reap the whirlwind.

The population did not reach one billion until 1867. Yet, by 1935 there were two billion people; by 1965 it rose to three billion, and by 1975, four billion.

POPULATION EXPERT: Dr. Tom Calhoun

ECOLOGY EXPERTS: Dr. Stevens (bottom left),
Stuart Udall (top right), and Dr. Wursten (bottom right).

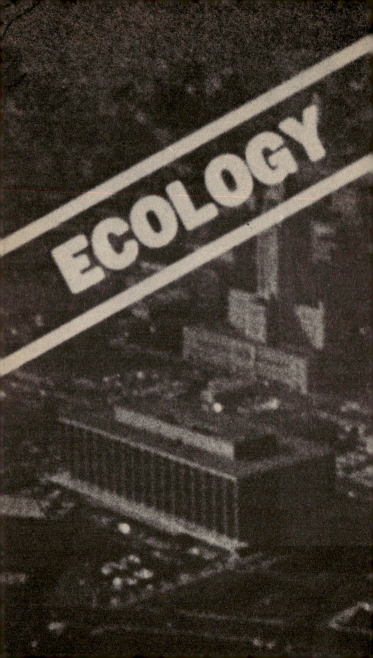

Dr. Tom Calhoun:

We're very close to a time early in the next century when it would be possible, if this process continued, for the total world population to double in twenty years. Well, you wouldn't have to continue this very much longer before the population would be doubling in twenty minutes.

Dr. Stevens (Federal Task Force):

Ozone is a minor but extremely important constituent gas in the stratosphere. Stratospheric ozone screens harmful ultraviolet radiation from the earth's surface. It is, therefore, principally the potential effects of increased harmful ultraviolet radiation, such as skin cancer and biological and agricultural effects, that are of concern.

Stuart Udall (former Secretary of Interior):

DDT is what you might call the uninvited additive. It is in man's food chain. It's in the ecosystem of the planet, and it poses a threat both to the environment and to man himself.

Dr. Wursten
(Chairman, Environmental Defense Club):

We now find that DDT residues have accumulated in both marine as well as fresh-water fish. So, we have to conclude that some major fisheries are threatened, both fresh water and marine. From an environmental standpoint, this is an extremely serious situation.

The environment has been giving us warnings and serving as a monitor for a long time, and in many

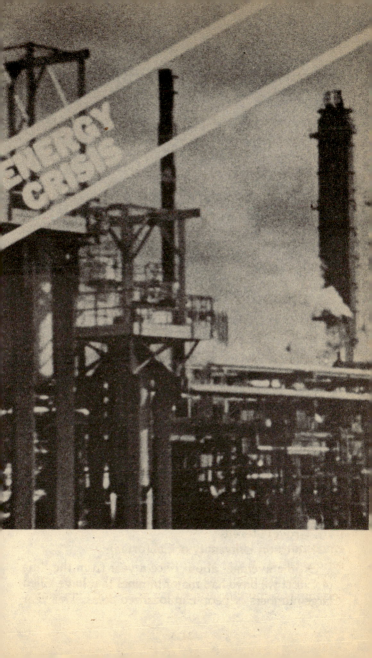

ways we haven't heeded those warnings.

Chuck Smith:

Another of the major concerns today is the energy supply on the planet Earth. As man is using up the fossil fuels, which cannot be replaced, he is turning more and more to the use of atomic fuels. These also pose a problem to the survival of man in finding a safe way to dispose of the waste materials that are still highly radioactive.

Solar energy has often been suggested as a viable alternative. But, with the billions of dollars and also the time needed to develop this resource, it is extremely doubtful if it can be ready in time to avoid disaster.

When the Age of Industrialization came, it seemed to promise man a utopia, a way to improve the quality of life on the earth. The need for fuel necessary to run this industrial complex can be the very thing that will destroy man, as it eats up all of his natural resources.

Another specter haunting man is the dwindling food supply. With the population increasing so rapidly and two-thirds of the world already suffering from malnutrition, the scientists who have studied this problem are quite concerned about the next 20 years, when they anticipate that the present population will have doubled.

Dr. Grover Stevens
(Professor, University of California):

On the average, about once a year from the time of Christ we have had major famines that have killed large numbers of people in localized areas. This year

FAMINE EXPERT: *Food demands continue to increase at a greater rate than food supplies, according to Dr. Grover Stevens of the University of California.*

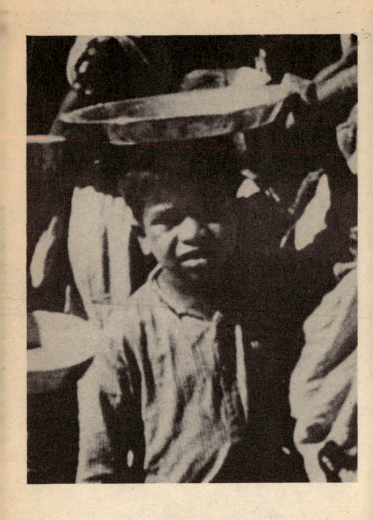

[1978] there will be 120 million new individuals born. Roughly 15 million will die before they reach the age of five through causes that are related to inadequate food. That represents one-third of the total death rate that will occur this year. Forty-eight million people will die; 15 million of them will be babies who die because of malnutrition.

The situation is even more grim and more tragic than that. One of the most important forms of under-nutrition and malnutrition is the failure of the child to get adequate protein resources to support his growth during his very early childhood development. If this happens, then the brain simply does not develop normally. These children grow up per-manently stunted in their mental capacities. Seven of ten are permanently stunted because of failure to ob-tain adequate sources of protein.

What are the prospects for improvement of this situation? Not particularly good. Supplies of high quality protein are not increasing as demand in-creases. This is a very diffcult thing to perceive. It is not an obvious phenomenon, but it is probably the most important cause of death across the world at the present time.

Dr. Henry Gainey, M.D.:

We have not been routinely immunizing against smallpox since 1971, because there's been no smallpox here [United States] for years. Therefore, each year there were more complications from the immunizations, and no one was getting smallpox—so it was decided that it was unwise to immunize peo-ple. So, soon we'll see a whole generation of unim-munized people, and the prospect of enemy action

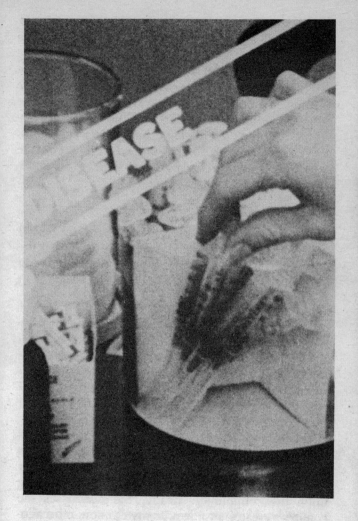

example, the brain tissue is very soft. Yours is the task to
grasp clearly the sharp line which separates a fine train
of reasoning from a false one.

seeding smallpox virus into our atmosphere is quite frightening.

Dr. Ira Abelow (Edgewood Arsenal, Maryland):

The fact is that a biological agent, when used according to certain doctrines, can have a very devastating and final effect on the personnel on whom it's used. The biological agent is a very large coverage weapon. It can be sprayed from aircraft. It can cover a very, very large area, and it can infect very many people in that area.

Chuck Smith:

There are also grave concerns about the social upheavals in our society. It is not surprising that the crime, which is another severe problem, is increasing more rapidly among the children and teenagers than any other age group.

Ed Davis (former Chief of Police, L.A.P.D.):

The American nuclear family—the mother, the father, and the children working together as an integral unit—has been disintegrating in our country. And this disintegration is costing us a terrible price. It isn't just the sufferings from crime.

Crime, of course, is essentially a youthful phenomenon, and the crime-prone age group tends to move down now to where the median age for burglars happens to be around 14 or 15, depending upon the community. Really, the reason it's the country's greatest problem, in my opinion, is because it really comes from a breakdown in the American family. Why do we have one out of two marriages

Dr. Henry Gainey (top) and Ira Abelow (botton) warn of potential plagues and diseases.

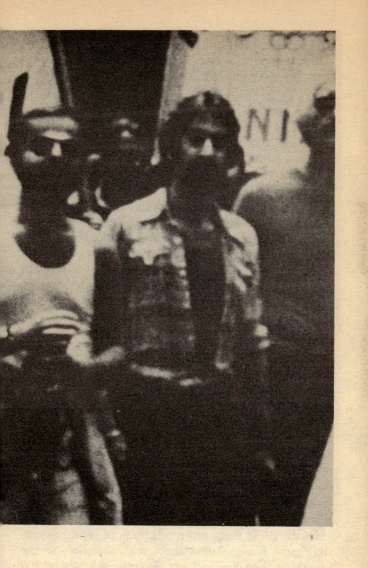

breaking up today? I think the morality of the American people has been shattered by the new morality, so-called situation ethics.

Chuck Smith:

Because of man's desperation, he has become prey to all kinds of false messiahs who offer non-reason religious experiences as a solution to his dilemmas. It is always startling to observe the incredible lies man will believe once he has rejected the truth.

One of the most awesome of nature's phenomena is the earthquake. It is a helpless feeling when that which is thought to be *terra firma* suddenly begins to move under your feet. Earthquakes have been increasing in the last century at an alarming rate. In 1975 there were more major earthquakes than in any other year in history. Almost three-quarters of a million people were killed that year by earthquakes.

I am not here to give you a story of doom. I am convinced that, in spite of all the gloomy forecasts by the social scientists and environmentalists, the world is on the verge of the most glorious age that man has ever known!

All of these things that have been happening on our planet—the famines, earthquakes, pestilences, the world wars, the false messiahs—are events that were predicted by Jesus Christ as signs of the end of man's futile efforts to govern himself.

In the Bible there are predictions of world events that must have seemed absolutely incredible to the people of that day and age. Even as recently as 200

Chuck Smith: "Man has come to the end of his time."

years ago, many men scoffed at the predictions. The prophet Daniel, 2500 years ago, said that in the last days there will be an increase in man's knowledge and technology to the extent that man would be traveling around the world.

Two hundred years ago the famous French philosopher, Voltaire, speaking of Sir Isaac Newton said, "Look at the mighty mind of Newton! When he got in his dotage he began to study the book called the Bible. And it seems, in order to credit its fabulous nonsense, 'We must believe,' says Newton, 'that the knowledge of mankind will be so increased that we shall be able to travel at 50 miles an hour.' The poor dotard!" Brilliant men like Voltaire mocked the men of faith. And yet, we see that Newton's faith has been substantiated, whereas Voltaire's criticism now seems foolish.

From a biblical standpoint, one of the reasons I believe that man has come to the end of his time is the rebirth of the nation Israel. It is an event that was predicted by most of the Bible prophets and by Jesus Christ, Himself.

As He gave the signs of the last days, He told His disciples that when the fig tree began to bud forth, they would know that summer was nigh. "Even know," He said, "My coming is at the door." Then Jesus said that that generation would not pass until all of these things be fulfilled [Matthew 24:32-34]. So, the rebirth of the nation Israel marks the final generation of man upon the earth in this present order.

And God sent Ezekiel into a valley that was full of dry bones and scattered. God said to Ezekiel, "Can

JERUSALEM! In 1967 the Israeli army occupied the

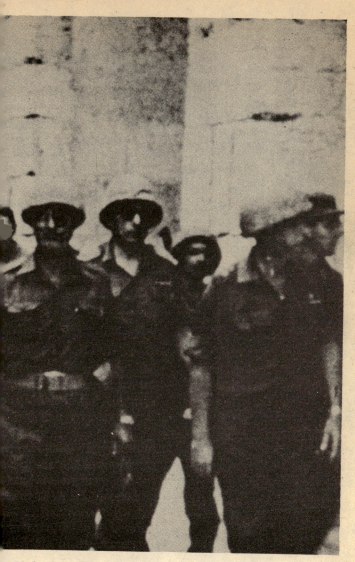

Holy City. Israel has controlled Jerusalem ever since.

Chuck Smith: "Here we see the fulfillment of God's wonderful Word!"

these bones be made to live again?"

Ezekiel said, "Lord, Thou knowest," and he watched as these bones came together. They formed a skeleton, and then flesh came upon this skeleton, and muscles.

God said, "And so shall I gather again My people Israel that have been scattered among the heathen, and I will bring them back into their own land, and I will establish them there" [Ezekiel 37]. So, God has kept this ancient promise to His people. He has brought them back into their land. He has established them there. We saw the miracle of a nation born in a day! [Israel became a nation on May 14, 1948.]

————————

We're standing across from the Knesset, which houses the Israeli government. And here we see the fulfillment of God's wonderful Word!

Jerusalem the Golden. Jerusalem the Eternal City, the city of ancient and modern charm. "For Jerusalem is a city," David said, "that has been joined together" [Psalms 122:3]. The Scripture actually means that people have come together within Jerusalem. Here we see an interesting blend of Arab and Israeli alike living side by side. The word in the Hebrew [*chabar*] actually means where people of all races can come together.

Behind us is the Western Wall, which to the Jew is one of the most sacred places in the world; for just beyond this wall was Solomon's Temple, exactly where we do not know. But yet, there at one time was the Holy of Holies, the place where God dwelt in the midst of His people.

This is as close as they [the Jews] can come to that

holy place. Since 1967 they have now been able once again to come and offer their prayers here at the Western Wall. It used to be called the Wailing Wall, because they were not allowed here by the Arabs. But, now that it is under Jewish control once again, they can come and, once more, worship their God in this sacred place.

Moshe Dayan (Foreign Minister):

As Jewish people, we have no other alternative but to try time and again to get peace.

Israeli Citizen:

These people are demonstrating . . . I can say it in

one word, for peace. Our will to fight is not something which can exist forever; because if our army, our people, and parents who have to send their children to the front, know that every victory leads to defeat—that means every military victory bought with blood leads to political defeat—there will be an end to it.

Menahem Begin (Prime Minister):

We have had all the experience with guarantees—since the Locarno Pacts [1925], and the guarantee to Czechoslovakia after Munich [1938], and the Tripartite Declaration in the early '50s for the Middle East . . . .

Israeli Citizen:

This time we have to be prepared, more than anytime else.

Menahem Begin (Prime Minister):

I would like to say, in simple words, that in the whole world there is no guarantee which can guarantee an international guarantee.

Moshe Dayan (Foreign Minister):

I think that all of us belong to the same kind of people. I don't really believe that ever there was ever a Jewish generation that was not worried, and was not worried about what will happen with the Jewish people at that time and in the future.

. . . We shall keep our artillery there, we shall keep our anti-aircraft guns there, and we shall keep our soldiers there along the Jordan River. Not in order to impose ourselves on these Palestinian Arabs. We don't want to do that. We are not an occupation, but we want to defend Israel, to take care of ourselves— which, unless we do that, no one else will do that for us.

Chuck Smith:

Here we see a tiny nation in the pains of birth . . . while in Europe one sees an interesting formation of ten nations federating together to form the European Community [EC], which is a fulfillment of biblical prophecy.

It is incredible to realize that the building that I am sitting in front of [EC headquarters in Brussels] has the potential of fulfilling a prophecy that was made

MODERN EMPIRE: Chuck Smith in front of the
European Community (EC) building in Brussels.

UNITED EUROPE: *The European Community, a*

fulfillment of biblical prophecy.

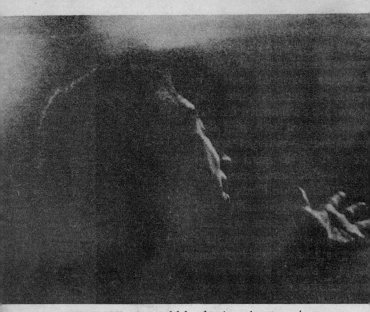

ANTICHRIST: A world leader is going to arise . . .

over 2500 years ago. This prophecy is recorded in the Book of Daniel.

We read that Nebuchadnezzar was King of Babylon, the first major world-governing empire. One night before he went to sleep, he was wondering, "What is to become of the world? What will become of my empire? What will follow after me?" That night he had a very interesting dream. The dream troubled him extremely.

When he woke up in the morning, he could not remember the dream, and he was curious as to its meaning. And so he gathered together his wise men and counselors, but they were not able to help him. Finally, Daniel was brought in.

Daniel said unto the king, "God has shown to you the kingdoms of the world, those empires that will govern this world. In your dream, you saw a great image. It had a head of gold. It had shoulders of silver. It had a stomach of brass. [It had legs of iron,] and feet [and ten toes] of iron and clay."

Daniel said, "Nebuchadnezzar, you are the head of gold. But your empire is to be replaced by the Medo-Persian empire, the shoulders of silver. That empire, in turn, will be replaced by the Grecian empire, the stomach of brass. That, in turn, by the Roman empire, the legs of iron. The final world-governing empire will be a federation of European nations that are related to the Roman empire, but they will be joined together in a democratic union." In the European

THE TEN: *Member nations of the European Community display their flags outside EC headquarters.*

Chuck Missler: The federated nations of Europe have grown from America's economic partner to a major competitor.

Community we find the potential for the final world-governing empire, the "ten toes."

We see already there are nine European nations that have federated together. Greece has made application and has been accepted. The treaties will be ratified within the next two years [by 1980], and you will find that there will be ten European nations joined together—represented by the ten flagpoles here in front of the building that headquarters the European Community.

But you'll notice that there is an eleventh flagpole here. That flagpole, we believe, will be for the leader that is to arise. A leader is going to arise to rule over the European Community that will almost hypnotize people. He will speak of peace, and the world that is searching for survival will hail him as their Messiah. However, the Scriptures warn us that he is a false messiah, for he is called the Antichrist by the Word of God.

We see this building which houses the European Economic Community— and here is the potential for the fulfillment of these prophecies!

Chuck Missler (Corporation President):

In 1951 under the Kennedy round of negotiations, it was the posture of the U.S. government to encourage the formation of the European Community so as to have a strong Atlantic partner to help defend the free world. Today, we're becoming aware of the fact that we have not so much a partner as a very able competitor.

We have special studies that are exploring the takeovers of U.S. companies and banks by European interests. We have feature articles in some of our media. "Europe, America's New Rival" [*Time*]. We have *Forbes:* "Is U.S. Technology Failing: Who now builds a better mouse trap?" *Business Week:* "Where U.S. technology competes—and doesn't."

Our basic productivity is being challenged. The potential industrial might of Europe is more than twice as large than the Soviet Union and perhaps 30 or 40 percent larger than the United States.

There's also a parliament that meets. I don't mean a parliament in Germany, or France, or Britain. I mean a European Parliament. It's only one step from there to control increasing budgets and, in effect, to have a federal government.

Slowly, we've become aware of the fact that this Treaty of Rome [1957] isn't just a customs treaty. It is the foundation document for a federal government of Europe. Shortly, we'll have ten nations in Europe under a consolidated federal leadership that will control the economic heartland of the planet Earth and form the principle economic competitor to the interests of the United States and the companies that are based here.

Chuck Smith:

What is happening to the dollar is of great concern to the average American family today. The dollar is devaluating on the foreign markets, and its purchasing power is diminishing in the United States.

There is also the problem in the use of money itself—especially in all of the crimes where money is the primary object stolen. The ideal answer is the credit card, where with a coded number on a card you can buy and sell. By issuing a card that will be

NEW ECONOMY: *The world's financial computer center is located underground at the World Trade Center in Brussels.*

SWIFT: Spokesman for The Society for Worldwide
Interbank Financial Telecommunications (SWIFT)
Erick O'Brien.

placed in the computer, there can be made an automatic transfer of the funds from the individual's account to the market's account.

The problem with the card, ultimately, lies in the identity—making sure that the person using the card is the authorized user. Solving this problem is of grave concern to the banking industry. Most felons arrested today have several stolen credit cards on their person, because they find that they are able to transfer these stolen cards quickly into cash or goods.

A solution that has been suggested is to assign every individual a number that will be tattooed onto the skin of his hand or upon his forehead, perhaps by laser beam. The world is now coming very close to that moment when the Scripture will be fulfilled which tells us that no man can buy or sell except he have a number on his right hand or on his forehead [Revelation 13:16-17]. Electronic funds transfer [EFT] is not around the corner. It is here, now!

We are now in Brussels, and behind me the impressive building is the World Trade Center. And in this building, two floors underground, there is a Burroughs computer that has been designed to transfer funds from the major banks throughout the world.

The security system surrounding this computer is, perhaps, one of the most sophisticated in the world; for this computer controls the transfer of billions of dollars each week between the major banks of the world. It is interesting that this computer is in Brussels, the city which presently is the capital of the European Community.

Erick O'Brien (Services Director for SWIFT):
Very briefly, a few forward-thinking members of

our community, the international banking operations community, in 1969 conceived the concept that we now know as SWIFT. Having elicited a sufficient level of support from the international banking operations community, SWIFT, as we now know it, was formed: The Society for Worldwide Interbank Financial Telecommunications (Société Cooperatif), headquartered here in Brussels.

Those of you who have been close to it recognize the magnitude of the development that we have accomplished. We are now at 503 member banks in 17 different countries and are operational in the first 15 countries, which represent our Phase I bank-connection exercise.

Chuck Smith:

We realize that each bank which is connected into this computer is also connected by computer relays to the local stores—so that the equipment and the technology necessary to establish the system of buying and selling with numbers has already been developed and is now operational.

Erick O'Brien (Services Director for SWIFT):

Later this afternoon at the Club Galloise, Prince Albert will officially inaugurate our system.

Prince Albert:

I, Albert, Prince of Belgium, declare the SWIFT system officially open in the hope that this forward step in international communication will reflect itself in growing international understanding and cooperation throughout your membership and the world.

Prince Albert: In 1977 the Prince of Belgium inaugurated SWIFT.

Chuck Smith:

This interbank fund transfer system has the potential of fulfilling another amazing Bible prophecy.

Though there is a tremendous potential for the European nations to become a world-governing empire, they will never rise to that stature until something is done about the great threat that Russia poses to Western Europe. It was reported in one of the national magazines recently that Russia has over 28,000 tanks in Eastern Europe ready to strike [*Reader's Digest*, July 1977]. Our own intelligence agencies believe that Europe will fall within 36 hours from the time of Russia's initial attack. Therefore, we have no hope of holding Europe against this massive Russian force. Thus, in order for Western Europe to ever be a world-governing empire, something must be done about this Russian threat.

Interestingly enough, the Bible states that Russia will be destroyed in an abortive invasion of Israel. In all the recent wars, and especially the 1973 Yom Kippur War when Israel fought for its very survival, Russia was deeply involved.

When the Syrians began their attack on October 6, 1973, they had some of Russia's latest equipment, such as this T-62 tank; and with 1,800 tanks they attacked across this upper end of the Golan Heights in a 20-mile battle perimeter. When we stop to realize that when Hitler began his great invasion of Russia, he had 1,000 tanks over a 200-mile perimeter, we realize what an intensive attack that was.

A few hours after the attack began at two [o'clock]

T-62: The Syrians attacked Israel in 1973 with 1,800 tanks, including Soviet T-62s, over a 20-mile battle front.

(left)
KREMLIN-CAIRO ALLIANCE:
*In 1971 Soviet President
Podgorny (left) and Egyptian
President Sadat signed a
friendship and cooperation treaty
which legitimized Soviet
penetration of Egypt.*

(below)
SOVIET-SYRIAN ALLIANCE:
*Soviet President Brezhnev (center
left) with Syrian President Assad
(center right). Moscow supplies
Syria with arms and military
advisors.*

ON GUARD: In 1973 "the Israelis were forced once

again to fight for their lives."

in the afternoon, the Russian planes began to bring fresh supplies to both Syria and Egypt. The Russian technicians had trained the Egyptians and the Syrians. Few people realize how much Russia was involved in the 1973 war against Israel. Three days before the war began, Russia put two spy satellites into orbit in order to film the battle conditions.

A lieutenant in the Israeli army told me of the capture of Russian troops on the Golan Heights. When the tide of battle turned against Egypt and Syria and the forces of General Sharon had trapped the Third Egyptian Army, the first ones to know that the Third Army was trapped were the Russians. This knowledge they received through their spy satellite. It was then that Russia began to press for a cease-fire.

At 10:45 in the evening of October 24th, [Soviet Ambassador] Dobrynin came to [U.S. Secretary of State] Kissinger with a message from [Soviet Communist Party Secretary] Brezhnev. This note has

BY SURPRISE: The 1973 Yom Kippur War, launched by the Arabs on Israel's holiest day, caught the country by cruel surprise.

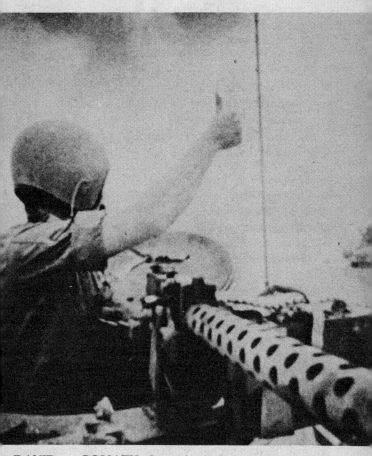

DAVID vs. GOLIATH: Soviet-backed Arab armies attacked Israel in 1967 and 1973. Israel has fought and won four wars in 25 years of existence.

been described by those who read it as brutal and threatening. According to the officials who read it, the content was, "We strongly urge that we both send forces to enforce the cease-fire, and, if you do not, we may be obliged to consider acting alone."

It is reported that Russia was loading paratroopers in the planes ready to invade Israel, and troopships were on their way. 1973 was almost the end!

President Nixon reacted to the note by calling a worldwide alert for our American forces. He probably averted World War III—because a cease-fire was soon decided upon, and the Middle East settled again into an unsteady peace.

The Israelis were forced once again to fight for their lives and for the right to exist in this little piece of land.

ISRAELI LEADER: Prime Minister Golda Meir held office from 1969 to 1974.

Golda Meir (former Prime Minister):

The Soviet Union, to our mind, is at least as responsible as the Arab countries, as Egypt is, for the Six-Day War [1967]. It is actually a party to the war. In what way? [Granted,] their personnel, their army, or their air force did not participate actively. But, in the first place, all the arms are Soviet arms, to Egypt especially and to Syria. They knew exactly what they are supplying these countries with arms for.

Moshe Dayan (Foreign Minister):

The role of Soviet Russia here [in the 1973 war] was to push the Arab world against Israel with the idea to destroy Israel. That's what they've been doing here for 20 years, ever since '57. Nothing else!

Joram Hamizrachi (Israeli Correspondent):

Russia was involved, no doubt about it. Russia threatened to take an active part in the war—in the last stage of the war when Israeli troops fought in Africa and endangered the Egyptian capital—Russia threatened to send troops, paratroopers, airborne troops, to fight in the Middle East. Russia sent airplanes to the Arabic countries. Russian freighters brought fuel supplies, ammunition—everything to the Arabic countries.

So, Russia was, no doubt, a part of the fighting parties here, although Russian soldiers didn't fight against us. But we found, after the war and during the war, enough proof to know that in some stages before the war in each Egyptian battalion there were Russian officers, in terms of advisors or in terms of army officers taking the command now and then. So, we were fighting, of course, also against Russia.

Chuck Smith:

We are presently on the Golan Heights, the area that was controlled by Syria prior to 1967. As we look at these gun emplacements and bunkers up here, we realize that this area was really a great area for what the Syrians were using it for. Now the Syrians would like it given back to them, and they are using the dollars from the oil in order to put pressure on the politics of government, in order that they might regain this territory that cost so much.

From this position the Syrian spotters were able to direct the artillery fire on the farmers down below. What a tragic thing that this beautiful territory had to be turned into a hell.

These are the Syrian bunkers and trenches that were constructed above the Hula Valley in the Golan Heights. They cost a lot of man-hours and a lot of man-dollars to develop, and they were purchased at the price of Israeli blood.

The major problem in the Middle East is that, now that the Israelis have transformed the wilderness into a Garden of Eden, the Arabs want it for a Palestinian state. This has become the stalemate in peace negotiations in the Middle East. The whole situation is a sad drama of political intrigue; because the Russians are using the Syrians to fulfill their end, and the Syrians are using the PLO [Palestine Liberation Organization] to fulfill their end—and Israel is the victim of these vicious attacks.

It does not seem that peace is just around the corner. The positions of the opposing sides have polarized so that it seems impossible for them to resolve

WEST BANK: The mayor of Ramallah seeks a return to Arabic control of the West Bank, occupied by Israel since 1967.

the differences. It is difficult to say just when the talks will break down completely, and they will try again to resolve their differences by another war. The Arabs talk so much about the right of the Palestinians to live in honor. It is obvious that the Palestinian situation has only been created to give the Arab nations an excuse for their next attack against the nation Israel, in their determined effort to destroy it.

Mayor of Ramallah (West Bank):

We, as Palestinians . . . Begin and his government, they should know that there'll be no peace in the area if the Palestinian will not be a part in any negotiations.

Moshe Dayan (Foreign Minister):

We do not want to accept the idea that Israel should go back from the [occupied] territories to the old line [pre-1967], and that there should be a Palestinian entity which eventually will turn into a Palestinian state. And we don't want to sit down with the PLO; and we are not going to sit down with the PLO, and we are not going to negotiate over a Palestinian state. Not that we are not going to agree about it. We are not going to negotiate about it!

Yasser Arafat (PLO):

You have to remember that in 1947 you vote for the [UN] Partition Resolution of my home country, my homeland, Palestine, for two states—Jewish state and Arab state.

Yasser Arafat: Leader of the Palestine Liberation Organization, which was recognized as the "representative of the Palestinian people" by the UN in 1974.

HUMAN RIGHTS: Joram Hamizrachi (right) explains the history of the Palestinian problem to Chuck Smith.

Joram Hamizrachi (Israeli Correspondent):

I'm ready to show you my birth certificate. My birth certificate was issued by the government of Palestine, authorized by His Majesty the King, the British King. I was born Palestinian, although Jewish. My father, when he joined the British army in the Second World War to fight against Nazi Germany, he joined as a Palestinian soldier. And the badge on his shoulder was saying, "Palestine." So, first of all, nobody gave them [the PLO] the right to decide that they are the only Palestinians.

Yasser Arafat (PLO):

You are obliged to recognize the Palestinian.

Joram Hamizrachi (Israeli Correspondent):

They had the possibility in 1948 to declare an Arabic State of Palestine, or whatever name, a PLO State, or whatever name which they have in their mind. But they did not do it, because Arabs, Jordanians, stole their rights, not Israelis.

Many Palestinian refugees ran into Arabic countries. I feel sorry for them. I feel sorry for every human being in need, and I don't make any difference whether he is Jewish, Moslem, or Christian. But, I'm sorry to say, that their brothers don't feel sorry for them; because those people who kept them in refugee camps in terrible conditions in Jericho or in southern Lebanon or in northern Lebanon or in Iraq or wherever, they kept them in a refugee camp as animals in a zoo or as dummies in an exhibition.

Every man has the right to live. Every man has the right to be sovereign of his country. Every man has the right to vote. Every man has the right to live as he

understands life. But the minute that, in talking for
human rights, you are destroying other lives and you
are killing, you are murdering, and you are butch-
ering people just because they don't agree with your
political terms—is it a pro-Russian motive or pro-
Israeli motive, a pro-American motive or a pro-
Cuban motive—I can't stand them! But let us try to
find out what *kind* of human rights—the right to live,
the right to live in honor, the right to educate your

*HOVELS &
HUTS: Many
"forgotten"
Palestinians
lived in these
now-abandoned
refugee camps
from 1948 to
1967.*

children as you like to educate them, the right to believe in God . . . .

Chuck Smith:

One of the sad and heartbreaking by-products of war are the refugees. The wars in Israel are no exception to this.

We are now in a Palestinian refugee camp that was built for the Palestinians by the Arabs after the 1948 war. They allowed them to live in these hovels for over 19 years, not really concerned or caring for them when they had opportunity. One wonders, why weren't the Arabs more concerned with the Palestinians at that time? Why so much concern now? There can be only one answer. It isn't really a concern for people. It's only a matter of politics.

David Oren (Israeli Reservist):

Should another war occur between Arab and Israel—which we expect anyhow because we don't know what will happen—my feeling is that this time we'll have to put an abrupt end to such a war, because we are all tired already from all the situations.

We are a state for 30 years. We live all the time under the pressure of a threat of war, and it's not easy to live this way. Because, you know, we are human beings like everybody else. We have our hopes, our dreams, our plans. When there is war every five, ten years, it's very hard to do all these things. If we'll be able to make a peace treaty now, then okay. Otherwise, there will be a war. We'll have to do it in such a way to make our maximum, that it will be the last [war]. We don't want to fight anymore. And we can't afford ourselves losing any war, because it will be the end of the State of Israel, and as Jews we know already what will happen to us here. We just pray and hope for the best in these matters. It's not easy.

Gen. Arik Sharon (Israeli):

The lesson of the last war was the Arab belief that they are running the risk [of defeat] if they would start an overall war. They believe that in order to destroy Israel step-by-step, gradually, they don't have to run this risk. For them it is enough for Israel to be in a situation where Israel cannot win a war, and/or the war cannot be a decided war.

Chuck Smith:

Should there be another Arab-Israeli war, there has been talk lately about the necessity of a decisive victory for the Israelis. Do you feel that this is what is going to have to happen?

Joram Hamizrachi (Israeli Correspondent):

I think there is no other choice. I don't trust politicians. I don't trust Russian politicians; I don't trust American politicians. I trust only myself, and because I trust only myself—I'm talking about myself, I mean my Israeli brothers and everyone in Israel—we have to make the decisions. One of those decisions might be the decision to attack first, in order to knock out their aircraft on the ground, to knock out their tanks in their storage, in their depots—not to wait until they roll over the border fence and cross into the Golan Heights or Sinai or even the plains of Judea. You have to knock them out before they will do it, if you know they are going to attack you.

Perhaps, we will have also to make brave decisions towards peace on our own—to decide that we have to give up or surrender or give back some of the territories. Who knows? But this should be our decision, not the decision made by others. And, unfortunately, today the situation is that people sitting in Moscow or in Washington, they're trying to play the

game. They're trying to make the decisions.

If you take the possibility of Russians fighting against us, of course it is a possibility. Four years ago [1973] they threatened to send airborne troops into Israel to fight against us. What is it? It is a Russian invasion!

If they will make the decision to attack us, there is no technical problem for Russia to attack Israel. The Russian border is so close to Israel that, in terms of modern warfare, it is a matter of hours from making the decision to have your first Russian Cossack fighting against you in the Galilee and the Negev. But it won't mean that we will not fight against them. We will not welcome them.

Chuck Smith:

It is obvious that, when the war starts again, Israel, as she has determined, will carry the war outside her own borders. Russia, who almost invaded in 1973, will surely move to stop Israel's takeover of the Arab states and the vast oil reservoirs of the Middle East.

When Russia attacks Israel, the prophecies of Ezekiel 38 and 39 will be fulfilled, where God declares that He would bring Magog, the land of Russia, against this little nation, Israel. In the last days, the Bible declares, Russia will come with a tremendous army, joined by the forces from Eastern Europe, the Balkan states, Ethiopia, Libya, and the Arab states.

God says that at this time His fury will arise in His face and that He will destroy this invading army. The Word of God again declares that five-sixths of the invading army will be destroyed!

The carcasses will lie unburied for seven months.

ARMY OF MAGOG: *Five-sixths of the invading army will be destroyed, according to the prophecy of Ezekiel.*

GRIM REMAINS: *"I will give thee unto the ravenous birds of every sort, and to the beasts of the field to be devoured"* (Ezekiel 39:4).

GRAVES OF MAGOG: *The location of the skeletons will be marked, and*

professional buriers will go throughout the land burying the bones.

At that time, the Israelis will then begin to bury the carcasses. The Scriptures tell us that when a person finds a skeleton, rather than touch it, they will set a flag by it, and professional buriers will go through the land to bury the bones [Ezekiel 39:14]. In another prophecy, God states, "And this shall be the plague with which the Lord will smite all the peoples that have fought against Jerusalem: Their flesh shall consume on their bones, and their eyes shall consume away in their holes, and their tongue shall consume away in their mouth" [Zechariah 14:12]. These are the same effects that the neutron bomb would produce.

As we look around, we now understand what Jesus meant when He said, "Except those days be shortened, no flesh will remain upon the earth" [Matthew 24:22]. We see the necessity for these days to be shortened because of the super-weapons that man has developed that threaten to destroy this planet.

When the Russian army is destroyed by God as it invades Israel, the way will then be paved for the ten European nations to rise as the world-governing power. Their new leader will inaugurate the new monetary system, based on buying and selling with an assigned number. And the world will enter the final countdown!

Almost 2,000 years ago God stepped out of eternity into time and walked with man whom He created. As He left the earth, He promised that He would return again to establish a kingdom of love, understanding, and peace. His coming again is essential for man's survival.

When His followers asked Him for the signs of His return, He told them the signs to watch for—the chief of them being the rebirth of the nation Israel. Against incredible odds, the nation Israel was born-again May 14, 1948. Jesus said the generation that saw the rebirth of the nation Israel would be the last generation.

Menahem Begin (Prime Minister):

Ours is almost a biblical generation.

Chuck Smith:

God would be fully justified if He just let man destroy himself. But, because He loves, He has promised to intervene. All He asks is that you seek to know Him and love Him in return. Your suvival depends upon it.

———————

It is incredible to realize that the Bible speaks so explicitly of the world conditions today. Yet, as we look at history and see how accurately it predicted past events, we shouldn't be surprised.

One of the most astounding of all Bible prophecies is found in the Book of Daniel, chapter 9. When the angel told Daniel that from the time the commandment would go forth to restore and rebuild Jerusalem to the coming of the Messiah the Prince would be 69 sevens [7-year periods] or 483 years. The Babylonian calendar was predicated on a 360-day year. So, that would equal 173,880 days [483 years x 360 days=173,880 days].

Now, history tells us that on March 14, 445 B.C., Artaxerxes gave the commandment to Nehemiah to restore and rebuild Jerusalem. Exactly 173,880 days later, Jesus on April 6, 32 A.D., made His triumphant entry into the city of Jerusalem.

While He came here on the Mount of Olives He stopped, and looking over the city He cried, "O Jerusalem! Jerusalem! If you only knew the things that belong to your peace in this thy day" [Luke 19:42]. It was their day of salvation! "But," He said, "now are they hidden from your eyes. Your city is to be leveled, and your children are to be slain in your streets." And, as He saw that picture of destruction that would take place when Titus came in [70 A.D.], He wept over the city.

Zechariah tells us that He is coming again, and His foot will set in that day upon the Mount of Olives, and this mountain will actually split right in the middle [Zechariah 14:4]. And Jesus will then make His entrance again into the city of Jerusalem through this gate that is shut. For Ezekiel said that he saw the gate towards the east and it was shut; but, he said it is prepared for the Prince, that He shall enter in by that gate in that day [Ezekiel 44:2-3]. When He does, the Jew and the Christian alike will join together in hailing the Messiah as He establishes God's eternal Kingdom upon this earth.

Is there any hope for man's survival? Definitely. If you will receive Jesus Christ as your Saviour and Lord today, He will assure your survival.

"If you will receive Jesus Christ as your Saviour and Lord today, He will assure your survival."

ABOUT THE AUTHOR

CHUCK SMITH, a servant of the Lord Jesus Christ, has been a Bible teacher for more than 25 years. He is pastor of Calvary Chapel of Costa Mesa, California—an extensive teaching and evangelical ministry. His Bible commentaries have been instructional and inspirational to thousands of listeners. The Word For Today, a Christian cassette tape and radio program ministry, distributes these studies worldwide.

For a copy of our catalog, send your name and address to:
The Word For Today, P.O. Box 8000, Costa Mesa, CA 92626.

The 60-minute documentary *Future Survival* is available for broadcast television, on video cassette, and as a 16 mm film. For rental information, write to The Word For Today.